Infinite Riches

by
Catherine Harvey

Playdead Press

Published by Playdead Press 2012

© Catherine Harvey 2012

Catherine Harvey has asserted her rights under the Copyright, Design and Patents Act, 1988, to be identified as the author of this work.

A CIP catalogue record for this book is available from the British Library.

ISBN 978-0-9563749-7-4

Caution
All rights whatsoever in this play are strictly reserved and application for performance should be sought through the author before rehearsals begin. No performance may be given unless a license has been obtained.

This book is sold subject to the condition that it shall not by way of trade or otherwise, be lent, resold, hired out, or otherwise circulated without the publisher's prior consent in any form of binding or cover other than that in which it is published and without a similar condition including this condition being imposed on the subsequent purchaser.

Playdead Press
www.playdeadpress.com

CATHERINE HARVEY

Catherine was born in Liverpool and read English at Hertford College, Oxford, before studying Acting at the Central School of Speech and Drama.

Writing for theatre includes: at Theatre 503, *Broken Down*, *Building Walls* and *The Rialto Burns* (also Miniaturists at The Arcola and 503lab); *Mirror, Mirror* (Menier Chocolate Factory); *Face to Face* (Old Red Lion); *Sweet Dreams* (Comedians' Theatre Company at The Pleasance, Edinburgh); *Open Heart Football* (24:7 Festival, Manchester); *The Ash People* (Best Writer - Daffodil Theatre Awards and published in *The Good Ear Review*). Radio/audio drama includes: *Crocodile Tears* (read at The Comedy Project, Soho Theatre); *Dr Who: The Queen of Time* and *Dr Who: Recorded Time* (Big Finish Productions).

Catherine also works as an actor in theatre, film, TV, radio and voiceover, and directs new writing, stand up and sketch comedy. She is a member of the Finborough Theatre's Literary Development Ensemble, the Young Vic Genesis Directors Project and an Associate of London Classic Theatre.

Catherine won Best Writer at Redfest for *Angeldust*, and as a result was commissioned to write *Infinite Riches* for the Old Red Lion. It is her first full length stage play.

With thanks to:
My husband, Tom, for steadfastly undertaking this journey with me; Alex Chisholm at West Yorkshire Playhouse; Clare Slater at the National Theatre; Julia Tyrell; Louise Hill; Tom Mansfield at Upstart; Neil McPherson at the Finborough; Michael Cabot at London Classic Theatre; Sam Snape; Sofie Mason at OffWestEnd.com; Steve Harper at Theatre 503; Shani and the cast; and everyone at the Old Red Lion and Playdead Press. Especial thanks to the actors who worked on the R&D with me in the snow – Alan Drake, Eileen Nicholas, Charlotte McKinney and Zazie Smuts.

For my parents, who loved to laugh.

Infinite Riches was first performed at the Old Red Lion Theatre, London, on 15th May, 2012. The cast was as follows:

NAN: Lesley Stone
PHIL: Daniel Simpson
JULIE: Zazie Smuts
LINDA: Charlotte McKinney

Director: Shani Erez

Infinite Riches

by
Catherine Harvey

CHARACTERS:

NAN: as old as the hills

PHIL: late 30s/early 40s

JULIE: 20s

LINDA: late 30s

ACT 1

Prologue:

Nan, sits in a rocking chair. She is dressed in black, with a quantity of jewellery – gold chains and rings. A jeweller's eyeglass and a small notebook hang on ribbons round her neck. Beside her is a table from which a single Halloween lantern casts an eerie shadow around the darkened room. She talks directly to the audience.

NAN: Once upon a time there was this bloke. Funny fella. Big ears. Bit of a belly. And what he did... (*Laughs, shaking her head*) What he did - he made a set of wings – or he got someone else to make them 'cos he was a lazy git. (*Laughs*) Then he flew right off into the sky – no messing - over the sea, far far away. The people below him looked like tiny ants with their grubby jobs and their need and their pain. And he felt so good soaring high up there. He felt so good he kept on flying without a single thought in his big-eared head. What did he care if he went too near the sun! He'd designer shades and he fancied a tan. (*Laughs*) What did he care - he was free of it all! (*Beat*) His body grew light and the wind streamed through his hair. And the stupid sod was having the time of his life - so he didn't notice how warm it was getting. Until, that is, he started to fall. And when he fell, he fell and fell. He fell so fast it took his breath away. You see, it'd got so hot his wings had melted - and the big-eared bugger hadn't packed a parachute. (*Smiles*)

'Sympathy For the Devil' plays as lights fade and music crossfades into:

Interlude 1

Voiceover in darkness. Phones ring - calls to Phil's mobile, each one increasing in pace and intensity, overlapping until they form a mass of noise.

FEMALE 1: (*young, sweet*) Hello, can I speak to Mr Haven please?

PHIL: This is Phil Haven/

FEMALE 1: I'm calling from Barclaycard/

PHIL: (*cautiously*) Yes, hello?

MALE 1: Hi, I'm calling from British Gas.

FEMALE 2: I'm calling from Thames Water...

MALE 2: ...From Mastercard...

FEMALE 3: ...Marks and Spencer Money...

MALE 3: ...Nat West Bank...

PHIL: What's this about?

MALE 1: There appear to be some irregularities in your payments.

PHIL: Really?

FEMALE 1: (*apologetically*) I'm afraid your direct debits have been returned by the bank.

PHIL: I don't/understand...

MALE 2: Do you know why that might be?

PHIL: No, I/can't...

FEMALE 3: Did you want to make a payment over the phone/right now?

PHIL: Well, it's a bit difficult at the moment/you see my hours have been cut...

MALE 1: If you could just give us five hundred pounds/it would sort everything out...

PHIL: (*horrified*) Five hundred pounds! Where am I/ going to get..?

FEMALE 1: Perhaps if we set up a new direct debit/ it would stop this from happening again...

PHIL: I'm not sure I'll be able to get to the bank/today...

FEMALE 2: If you could give us your card/details...

PHIL: It's a very bad line. Can I call you back?

The noise of ringing phones swells – then stops abruptly. Nan nods and smiles, lit by the Halloween lantern. Lights fade to darkness.

Scene 1

A Park. Lunchtime. **Phil** *sits on a bench clutching his mobile phone like a cornered animal. He wears work trousers, shirt and tie under a leather jacket. He sniffs mournfully, coughs, and takes a sip of water from a plastic bottle that is half full - or half empty, depending* *on how you view the World. On his knee is a homemade sandwich wrapped in foil. Occasionally he throws a crumb to a passing duck as if he is throwing away pieces of his life.* ***Julie*** *enters. There is something otherworldly about her, and at moments we have a sense that a spell is being cast over Phil. She carries a carton of orange juice.*

JULIE: Why so glum, chum?

PHIL: Sorry?

JULIE: I could heal you.

PHIL: What?

JULIE: Of your glumness. This is your lucky day.

PHIL: Would you/(mind)...?

JULIE: I'm your guardian angel, innit. That's from Ancient Greek – 'angel'. Means messenger. (*Dramatically*) I bring you tidings of great joy. (*Smiles expectantly*)

Pause. ***Phil*** *looks at her then throws another piece of bread to the ducks.*

JULIE: Or were you meditating? 'Cos that's Latin

that is. Meditor, meditari, meditatus sum – to reflect upon, study, or to ponder. Was that what you was doing? Having a good old ponder?

PHIL: Do I know you?

JULIE: We was at school together.

PHIL: Right. (*Coughs, swigs the last of his water*)

JULIE: Back in the day.

PHIL: I see.

Julie sits on the bench beside him. Phil and Julie stare at the ducks. Phil coughs and throws another piece of bread. Julie points and hisses at a duck, then laughs to herself.

JULIE: They can be little fuckers can't they?

PHIL: (*deep in thought*) Yes... (*To her*) Who?

JULIE: Ducks.

PHIL: Oh... right.../I see...

JULIE: I like your jacket. Do you like my top? (*Shows him her top*)

PHIL: Are you chatting me up?

JULIE: You're way too old for me.

PHIL: I thought you said we were at school together. (*Coughs, looks at his bottle – it is empty*)

JULIE: (*offering the carton*) Juice?

Phil coughs, shakes his head.

JULIE: I haven't spat in it. But I can if it turns you on. (*Grins*)

Phil softens. Julie hands him the carton. Still coughing Phil takes it, drinks.

JULIE: That's a bad cold you got there. You wanna watch that.

PHIL: I will. Thanks.

JULIE: Echinacea.

PHIL: Sorry?

JULIE: It means spiny.

PHIL: Is there a point to this?

JULIE: Too right there is, 'cos a dose of that'd sort you out. I could get you some if you like. And Vitamin C. Won't cost you nothing.

PHIL: I'm fine, honestly.

JULIE: I'll even throw in a bottle of Buttercup Syrup. (*Makes a bowling gesture*)

PHIL: (*irritated*) No! (*Coughs, drinks*)

JULIE: You'll regret it 'cos that is well tasty flower juice. Believe.

PHIL: (*coughing*) Please... (*Coughing*) Would you/just...

JULIE: If you eat a buttercup it don't taste that good.

Beat. **Phil** *coughs.*

JULIE: How can you afford that?

PHIL: What?

JULIE: Your jacket.

Phil *looks down at his jacket. As he starts to speak*

Julie resumes –

JULIE: Ah, now you're sucking a lemon.

PHIL: No, I'm/not...

JULIE: I wasn't saying you was common...

PHIL: Please... (*Coughs*)

JULIE: But that is a properly expensive jacket.

PHIL: (*coughing*) Would you/just...

JULIE: I know the price of them bananas.

PHIL: (*confused*) What? (*Beat, coughs*) Look, would you just sod off. That's from Latin too - sodus offus. It means to leave me alone. To fuck right off through the park gates and not come back.

Beat. **Julie** *pretends to cry.*

JULIE: I was only... (*Sobs*)

PHIL: No, don't/do that...

JULIE: Trying to... (*Sobs*)

PHIL: Come here... (*Puts his arm around her*)

*They sit together for a while. **Julie** cries while **Phil** drinks orange juice awkwardly.*

JULIE: (*wiping her eyes*) You've got serious aggression issues. You should see someone about that.

PHIL: You shouldn't talk to strangers.

They laugh. Beat.

PHIL: Look, I have to.../you know... (*Stands*)

JULIE: What do you want most in the world? I can get it for you.

PHIL: Why?

JULIE: I'm your Guardian Angel, innit. This is your lucky day.

PHIL: (*hesitates, tempted*) I have to get back to work.

JULIE: Come on – what is it - (*acting them out*) Money? Power? (*Dramatically*) Sex?

***Phil** laughs.*

PHIL: You can't give me what I want – no offence, love.

JULIE: Go on. What's the worst that can happen?

*Beat. **Phil** coughs, then reaches into his pocket to find some change.*

PHIL: So, that Vitamin C – you reckon it works?

JULIE: My old Nan, she swears by it.

PHIL: Well then, I'd better get some.

JULIE: Echinacea too?

PHIL: (*looking doubtfully at his change*) I'm not sure/ I've enough...

JULIE: Stay right there. (*Turns to go*)

PHIL: No, I didn't/mean...

JULIE: I'll be back in a tick.

PHIL: No... (*Calls after, holding out the money*) Hang on - I haven't given you/any...

JULIE: (*calls*) I don't need your money, mate. I'm

like Hong Kong Phoey - quicker than the human eye. (*Does a karate chop*)

Phil *laughs.*

JULIE: You're gonna stay here, aren't you?

PHIL: Yeah.

JULIE: And wait for me?

PHIL: I said, didn't I?

JULIE: Cross your heart and hope to die – 'cos I'm not nicking you a load of healthy gear then finding you've fucked off without improving your sanity. (*Beat, thinks*) That's odd, innit? Sanity.

PHIL: Sorry…?

JULIE: Well, it's from sanis – which if you translate literally is like your physical health…

PHIL: If you say so.

JULIE: I think you'll find it is, even if I don't say so. It's one of them things that's just true. Like David Dimbleby.

Phil laughs.

JULIE: So, you staying here or what? 'Cos there's a lot of lies in this world and I don't see you crossing your heart.

PHIL: Cross my heart. (*Crosses his heart*)

JULIE: And?

PHIL: And hope to die. (*Puts his hand to his chest*)

JULIE: See, that didn't hurt, did it?

Julie exits. Phil waits until she is gone, then stands. As he is about to exit he takes a last swig from the carton of orange juice, looks at it, hesitates, then goes back and sits on the bench. His mobile rings – he glances at it, winces, then rejects the call. He continues to wait as the lights fade.

Interlude 2

Voiceover in darkness - advertisements overlap as if someone is retuning a radio.

VO1: Have you had an accident at work?/Then call... (*Radio is retuned*)

VO2: Play online Bingo and win these fabulous/prizes. (*Radio is retuned*)

VO3: And the final question for a jackpot of five hundred pounds – how many giraffes/... (*Radio is retuned*)

VO4: Do you want to turn your unwanted gold into much needed cash?

The volume on the radio is turned down into:

Scene 2

Phil and Linda's dining room. The same day – evening. In the darkness we hear Linda's voice.

LINDA: (*with sympathy, as if talking to a crying baby*) Ah! Did the nasty man on the nasty radio scare you? There you go... (*Sound of pouring water*) That's better, isn't it..?

The lights gradually fade up during the following, to reveal Linda sitting alone at a well-worn table, holding a glass of water and talking to a pot plant. On the table is a plate containing the remnants of a jacket potato and baked beans. Beside her on the floor are a quantity of Pound Shop bags. There is a set of shelves filled with healthy, well-cared for plants.

LINDA: You were a bit dry weren't you? You wanted a drink. Yes, you did. You wanted a nice drink 'cos you were thirsty wirsty, yes you were. Oh, look - you've still got a bit of dinner on you, Morris. (*Pulls a tissue from her sleeve, licks it and cleans the leaves of the pot plant.*) There's a good boy.

The front door opens. We hear Phil (offstage) coughing and repeatedly trying to close the door – it sticks. **Linda** *puts the tissue back up her sleeve.*

PHIL: (*offstage, calls*) Hello.

LINDA: (*not looking up from the plant, calls*) Hi.

Phil *enters. He is carrying a bottle of Buttercup Syrup, a packet of Vitamin C and a small vial of Echinacea.*

PHIL: That door's sticking again. (*Kisses Linda's head, then notices Morris*) He looks much better. (*Peers at the plant*) You been talking to him? (*Laughs*)

LINDA: No.

PHIL: (*leaning too close to the plant*) He's your favourite, isn't he - Morgan?

LINDA: (*picking up the pot and hugging it*) Morris. His name's Morris.

PHIL: I can't keep/up.

LINDA: Morgan died. (*Beat, she turns away to put the pot plant on the shelf*) Morris is a money plant...

Beat

PHIL: I know, love, I didn't/...

LINDA: Morgan was a spineless yucca.

Linda exits to the kitchen. A cheap plastic swing bin is visible in the doorway.

PHIL: (*noticing her plate on the table, calls*) Oh, you've (eaten)...

LINDA: (*calls*) It's half past eight, Phil.

PHIL: (*calls*) Right.

Pause. We hear pans/plates rattling. **Phil** *looks towards the kitchen, then puts the Buttercup Syrup, Vitamin C and Echinacea on the table and reads the back of the Echinacea packet.*

PHIL: (*calls*) Did you sell many today?

LINDA: (*pops her head in, nods towards the plants*) Ssh!

PHIL: (*whispers*) Sorry.

LINDA: (*whispers*) Joan at the garage (*mouths the words inaudibly*) bought a dozen geraniums and some cress.

PHIL: What?

Linda hold up 12 fingers then mimes flowers and cress, while Phil tries to decipher what she means.

PHIL: Twelve..?

Linda nods.

PHIL: That's good isn't it?

LINDA: Yeah.

Beat

LINDA: (*noticing the medicine*) You starting a chemist's shop?

PHIL: I've a cold coming. (*Coughs*)

LINDA: Well, be careful which way you cough. I've only just nursed him back to health after the episode with the baked beans.

Linda exits to the kitchen. Phil picks up the Vitamin C packet. He notices there is a phone number written on it. He glances at the shelf where Morris lours down at him.

PHIL: (*looks at Morris, coughs on him deliberately*) Smug bastard.

Linda enters carrying a plate containing a burnt jacket potato and congealed baked beans. Phil hurriedly moves away from Morris.

LINDA: Ah, were you talking to him?

PHIL: (*innocently*) Yeah.

LINDA: That's nice. (*She places the plate in front of him*)

PHIL: (*glances woefully at his plate*) Thanks. This looks... lovely. (*Coughs*)

LINDA: Don't start, Phil.

Linda begins unloading the Pound Shop bags - tins of own brand beans, plant food, seeds and a head massager. Phil eats, feigning enjoyment.

PHIL: Mmm...

Linda removes the head massager from its tube, sneaks up behind Phil and massages his head with it.

PHIL: (*spits out his beans, coughing*) Jesus Christ!

LINDA: It's a head massager.

PHIL: I can see that. (*Coughs*)

LINDA: An orgasm in a tube the girl said. (*Approaches him again with the massager*)

PHIL: (*avoiding her*) I'm eating my tea, Lind. (*Coughs*)

Linda puts the massager away. Phil coughs, reaches for Linda's glass.

LINDA: Not that one. (*Snatches the glass out of his hand*) Not unless you like Baby Bio. (*Laughs, pours the water into one of the plants on the shelf.*)

***Phil** watches, coughing helplessly. **Linda** exits to the kitchen, while **Phil** continues to cough and glare with hatred at the plants.*

PHIL: (*to plants*) One of these days... (*Coughs*) I swear to God... (*Coughs*) I'll... (*Coughs*)

***Linda** brings back a glass of water, takes the tube of Vitamin C out of the packet, opens it and drops a tablet into Phil's glass. It fizzes.*

PHIL: Thanks. (*Coughs*)

LINDA: (*glancing at the packet*) There's someone's mobile number on this.

PHIL: (*innocently*) Is there? (*Coughs*)

***Linda** holds out the Vitamin C packet.*

PHIL: (*casually glances at it*) Oh - must be Steve's from work.

***Phil** takes a sip of the Vitamin C, pulls a face.*

LINDA: Wait for it to dissolve. (*Takes the glass out of his hand*)

***Phil** stares mournfully at the glass, waiting for the*

Vitamin C to dissolve. ***Linda*** *reads the seed packets. Pause.* ***Linda*** *throws the packets onto the table.*

LINDA: Why is it I can make all these grow, but I can't... (*Tearful*) you know...

Beat.

PHIL: (*deciding to drink*) Sod it! (*He takes a swig of Vitamin C*) Do you want a laugh?

LINDA: Yeah - go on. (*Wipes her eyes*)

PHIL: This morning I clicked on a link that said 'earn more money' and gave the whole office a virus. (*Laughs, sips the Vitamin C*)

Linda *laughs weakly. Pause.*

LINDA: Shall I show you what I bought?

PHIL: Go on then.

Linda *runs to the bags, rooting through them like a child at Christmas.* ***Phil*** *picks up the empty Vitamin C packet, looks at the mobile number, then puts the empty packet on his plate with the rest of the debris and exits to the kitchen. Through the open door we see him throw the packet into the bin, then scrape the remains of his beans* *and potato on top of it.* **Phil** *re-enters, wiping his hands on a tea towel.*

LINDA: Well... I got the head massager... (*Holds it out*)

PHIL: (*dodging the head massager*) Yeah, that's great.

LINDA: Isn't it... (*Using it on her head*) And the beans, of course...

PHIL: (*woefully*) You know I like/Heinz...

LINDA: They're half the price. You'll have to learn to live with them. *(Takes a tube of Aloe Vera hand cream out of the Pound Shop bag, puts some on, then holds it up triumphantly)* And Aloe Vera! It's meant to work miracles.

LINDA/PHIL: (*together*) 'Allo, Vera!

They laugh.

PHIL: (*takes her hand*) You've lovely hands.

Beat. **Linda** *pulls her hand away and roots in a bag.*

LINDA: And this... (*Holds up a book – '101 Things to do Before You Die'*)

PHIL: (*reading the title*) 'A Hundred and One Things to do Before You Die.'

LINDA: I thought we could work our way through it.

PHIL: (*takes book from her, starts to flick through it*) I didn't know you were into fantasy.

LINDA: I can have aspirations. I've always wanted a fur coat - and a set of those Emma Bridgewater cups in different patterns like they do in 'Escape to the Country'.

PHIL: (*reading*) Go to a show at Sidney Opera House. Eat dinner at the top of the Eiffel Tower. Take your kids to Disneyland...

LINDA: Stop it...! (*She tries to take the book from him*)

PHIL: (*pulling away from her*) Oh, wait – here's a good one - (*reading*) Commit a minor criminal act. We could do that this weekend.

LINDA: (*snatches the book from Phil, almost knocking Morris over*) Mind the plants! (*She shoves the book into a carrier bag and exits to the hallway with the bag*)

Phil coughs, takes a sip of Vitamin C. He looks at the

glass then glances towards the bin. He goes to the bin, peers in tentatively, then starts pulling out bits of burnt potato skin and beans in an effort to find the Vitamin C packet. He eventually finally finds the packet and wipes it clean, revealing the phone number.

PHIL: (*to Morris*) What are you looking at?

Interlude 3

In darkness. Voiceover – a mobile rings and is answered.

PHIL: Hello?

STEVE: Hi, is that Phil?

PHIL: Yes.

STEVE: This is Steve.

PHIL: Steve?

STEVE: From Human Resources.

PHIL: Sorry... Yeah... Hi, Steve.

STEVE: I was just checking how you were.

PHIL: (*confused*) How I...? Oh... (*realising, starts to cough*) right... (*has an ostentatious coughing fit*) The doctor says it's a chest infection. (*Coughs*)

STEVE: Sorry to hear that, mate.

PHIL: I've got those whatsisnames. (*Coughs*)

STEVE: Antibiotics?

PHIL: That's it.

STEVE: Did he mention when you might be able to come back to work, 'cos we'll need a letter if it's gonna be more than three days?

PHIL: No, he didn't... (*Coughs*) He said it was quite bad though and that I should... (*Coughs*) I should... (*Coughs uncontrollably*) Sorry, I... (*Coughs*)

STEVE: Not at all mate, you sound awful.

PHIL: Bed rest... (*coughs*)

STEVE: Yeah, you take it easy, mate. Get well soon.

***Phil** hangs up – dialling tone.*

Scene 3

The Park. Afternoon, a few days later. Shop alarm and police sirens in the distance. **Phil** *and* **Julie** *run in, exhilarated, panting.* **Phil** *is clutching a pair of jeans,* **Julie** *a leather jacket. They both collapse on the floor breathless and laughing.*

JULIE: Fucking Hell!

PHIL: That was amazing.

JULIE: Believe.

They lie on the ground catching their breath.

JULIE: What d'you get?

PHIL: A pair of jeans! (*Holds them up in triumph, laughing giddily, coughs*)

JULIE: Steady, tiger, or you'll implode. That's from plodo, plodere/to...

PHIL: (*lies down, coughs, holding his chest*) You're right. I think I'm going to have a heart attack.

JULIE: It's well better than poppers.

PHIL: Yeah. (*Pause – he lies on the ground trying to catch his breath*) I can't believe I'm bunking off work.

JULIE: (*examining the jeans*) You get the right size?

PHIL: I feel sixteen again.

JULIE: They look a bit big to me.

PHIL: What?

JULIE: You should always try before you buy. 'Cos you can't take them back if they're wrong.

PHIL: (*holds the jeans up against his legs – they are obviously too long*) Shit!

JULIE: (*laughs*) Schoolboy error!

PHIL: No way!

JULIE: Put them on.

PHIL: Here?

JULIE: Why not?

PHIL: (*hesitates*) What the Hell!

Phil takes off his trousers. Julie wolf whistles.

PHIL: (*like a shy schoolboy, enjoying the attention*) Shut up!

Phil puts on the new jeans. They are obviously much too large and too long for him – like clown trousers. Julie laughs.

PHIL: (*in despair*) Ah, no!

JULIE: You could always roll them up. It's quite trendy I'm told – amongst the older gentleman.

PHIL: Piss off.

They laugh. Phil watches as Julie puts on the leather jacket. It fits her perfectly.

JULIE: What do you think?

PHIL: Lovely.

JULIE: (*talking to the jacket, stroking it affectionately*) I've had my eye on you for a long time, haven't I. Just waiting for the right moment to pounce. (*To Phil*) Normally they have some buff bloke guarding the door. He could outrun me easy. (*Laughs triumphantly*) I knew it was Christmas when I saw that old Grandad today.

PHIL: Grandad?

JULIE: The security guard. He was like forty or something.

Beat.

PHIL: (*gathering up his clothes*) I should be at work.

JULIE: (*grabbing his jeans*) Swotty botty...

PHIL: Give me my jeans.

Phil *tries to take the jeans.* ***Julie*** *holds onto them, playfully.*

JULIE: Don't be such a spoilsport...

PHIL: I'm serious... I don't want to lose my job. (*Beat*) Come on...

Phil *tickles her.* ***Julie*** *tickles him. A tickle fight ensues.*

PHIL: Ah! Get off. (*He falls on the floor laughing*)

Pause. They look at each other.

JULIE: I bet you ain't never been on a date like this.

PHIL: This isn't a date.

JULIE: Isn't it?

Beat. Phil's mobile rings. **Phil** *looks at phone, winces, rejects the call. The phone rings again.*

PHIL: (*looks at phone*) Shit! (*Rejects the call*)

JULIE: You got a stalker?

PHIL: Couple of unpaid credit cards, that's all. (*Laughs edgily*)

JULIE: They can be right bastards can't they. My friend Elaine, she couldn't answer the phone for years. Even told them her mum died just to get them off her back. They cancelled the penalty charge and everything that month, no questions asked. But there's only so many family members you can kill in the pursuit of interest free credit. (*Laughs*) In the end my Nan had to sort it out.

PHIL: Your Nan?

JULIE: Yeah, she helps people. You know, like Mother Teresa. If you want money, my Nan could lend you some.

PHIL: Thanks, but I don't think she'd have the sort of money I need.

JULIE: You'd be surprised. She saves. In jam jars and stuff. She don't trust banks.

PHIL: Wouldn't she mind?

JULIE: What she want it for? She's old innit. (*Tasting the words*) And infirm. (*Beat*) You got any jewellery or movables that won't be missed?

PHIL: I think Linda's got some bits she hardly ever wears. Why?

JULIE: Come on - we'll take a detour via your house.

PHIL: Won't your Nan think it's odd if we turn up out of the blue?

JULIE: Nah - get her a bottle of Tequila and she'll be your friend for life.

Phil's mobile rings. **Phil** *looks at it.*

JULIE: Put it on silent. (*Beat*) Go on – live dangerously.

Phil hesitates, and then switches his phone to silent.

Interlude 4

In darkness, as voiceover. Phones ring throughout, the calls and voices overlapping, building in pace.

MALE 1: Our records show you have unpaid bills for March.

FEMALE 1: April.

MALE 2: May.

FEMALE 2: I'm afraid after three months we're required to take legal action.

MALE 3: Perhaps you could pay a small amount as a gesture of good will - say, five hundred pounds.

FEMALE 3: One thousand.

MALE 1: Two thousand.

FEMALE 1: There is a danger your credit rating may be affected.

MALE 2: In that case I'm afraid we'll have to disconnect your supply.

FEMALE 2: We may be required to send in the bailiffs.

MALE 3: If you could pay.

FEMALE 3: Pay!

MALE 1: Pay!

FEMALE 1: Pay!

MALE 2: Pay!

Ringing phones and voices crescendo – they are stopped abruptly by the sound of knocking. We hear a voice message on Phil's mobile.

LINDA: Hi, Phil, it's me. This man came round after you left. Said he was from the Electricity. Anyway, there's been some sort of mix up with the direct debits. Can you give me a call when you get this? Thanks.

Click and dialling tone as the call ends.

Scene 4

Julie and Nan's house. Later the same day. **Nan** *sits in a rocking chair in semi-darkness. The room is a decaying mess, filled with cobwebs, piles of paper, jars of coins, and various bits of Halloween memorabilia – grotesque fairy lights, a skull, a devil's face on a jar, shot glasses with skulls on them, piles of violent/horror-based computer games, a CD player, books - OED, Latin and Ancient Greek dictionaries, The Arabian Nights - and a large container of lo salt. We hear a rhythmic creak as the chair rocks. It stops when* **Nan** *hears whispered voices offstage. Noise of a key in the lock. The door opens.* **Phil** *and* **Julie** *are lit by light from the corridor.* **Phil** *clutches a bottle of Tequila and a plastic bag containing some of Linda's jewellery.*

JULIE: (*entering*) Open Sesame!

PHIL: (*entering, peers nervously into the darkness*) You sure this'll be all right?

JULIE: I told you, Nan's a saint. (*Tries light switch*) Bugger! (*Tries another switch*) There - (*Halloween lanterns turn on, though their light is dim*) that's better.

Phil *looks around him doubtfully - skulls flicker, and plastic ghosts and devils change colour from red to blue to* *green. **Nan** pretends to be asleep in the chair, still as a statue amidst the debris. **Phil** does not see her.*

PHIL: I should go home...

JULIE: (*grabs him*) Don't be silly. (*Opens the curtain slightly*) Look! We've a great view of your mates, the ducks.

***Phil** opens the curtains wider – revealing the room in all its glory.*

PHIL: (*shocked*) Woah!

JULIE: Nan has a penchant for Halloween, innit.

PHIL: (*puts down the bag of jewellery and looks around*) You can say that again. (*Picks up a skull and examines it*)

JULIE: She says it keeps her connected with her imminent mortality. You know as in mors, mortis the death that is to come.

PHIL: She sounds a laugh a minute.

JULIE: She is.

*Scuttling noise. **Phil** drops the skull. The lights flicker.*

PHIL: What was that!

JULIE: Just Boris.

PHIL: Boris?

JULIE: Nan's pet rat. (*Beat*) I know - it's one serious indictment of the Conservative Mayor.

Squawking, flurry of wings from offstage.

NAN: (*waves her arms in the air, setting the chair rocking*) Pissing pigeons!

PHIL: (*shocked*) Shit!

JULIE: All right, Nan.

NAN: Pissing pigeons've ballsed up the electricity again.

PHIL: You wanna get yourself some netting.

NAN: (*irritably*) What's that?

JULIE: He says we should get some netting.

NAN: Who does?

JULIE: Phil.

NAN: Who the fuck's Phil?

PHIL: I am.

Nan looks him up and down. Phil becomes increasingly self-conscious.

NAN: Are you stopping?

PHIL: Sorry?

NAN: (*grandly*) Is this a flying visit or are you gracing us with your presence for an extended period of time?

Phil looks bemused.

JULIE: (*confidentially*) Take your jacket off.

PHIL: Oh... (*Takes off his jacket, looks round for somewhere to put it, but can't find anywhere. He coughs then grins nervously*)

NAN: Your lottery numbers come up last night?

PHIL: No..?

NAN: Then what you got to grin about?

Phil's face drops. Beat.

NAN: I'm only fucking with you.

*Nan and **Julie** laugh.*

PHIL: (*laughs uneasily*) Oh. Right. Nice one...

NAN: (*to Julie*) Not much to look at is he. (*Peers closer*) You must have hidden talents.

*Nan laughs dirtily, nudging Phil. **Phil** coughs.*

NAN: You wanna try Echinacea for that.

PHIL: Oh, I'm/already...

NAN: (*confidentially*) My Robert went like a steam hammer. That was his hidden talent. He's dead now, of course.

PHIL: I'm sorry for your loss.

NAN: Don't be, son. He was a cunt.

*Beat. **Phil** looks to Julie for help.*

JULIE: He was. He put it about.

NAN: But he got his comeuppance in the end. They all do.

Beat.

JULIE: Drink?

PHIL: (*relieved*) Please!

Julie holds out her hand for the bottle.

PHIL: Oh... right... Sorry... (*Hands Julie the Tequila*)

JULIE: Drink, Nan?

NAN: Mmm?

JULIE: Phil's brought Tequila. I thought we could do slammers.

NAN: Do barracudas shit in the woods!

Julie and Nan laugh uproariously at the in joke. Julie pours the Tequila into shot glasses – each has a skull on it. Phil puts his coat on the back of a chair.

NAN: Don't touch anything.

PHIL: Sorry... (*Picks up his coat*)

NAN: Everything's in order.

Phil looks round at the mess, bemused.

JULIE: (*handing him a glass*) Here.

PHIL: Cheers. (*As in 'thanks'*)

JULIE: Nan's wicked isn't she?

PHIL: (*looking around him*) Yeah...

Julie takes Nan her drink and a large plastic container of lo salt.

JULIE: Here you go, Nan.

NAN: Is there no lime?

JULIE: They didn't have none down the Co-op.

NAN: Fuck a duck! (*Salts her hand*) This neighbourhood's going to Hell in a handcart, Philip. (*Shakes her head, then raises her glass*) Arses ahoy!

Julie and Nan lick the salt on their hands, then down the Tequila in one and, racing to be the first to finish, slam their glasses on the table. Both look at Phil who is still holding his full glass.

PHIL: (*realising*) Oh... sorry... (*Tries the salt, pulls a face, then attempts to slam the Tequila, coughs*)

Julie and Nan laugh.

NAN: That'll put hairs on your chest. (*Laughs dirtily, refilling their glasses*)

PHIL: Thanks.

Julie puts on a CD - Lady Gaga's 'Poker Face' - and moves to the music, singing and occasionally making poking movements towards Phil's face when he catches her eye. Phil watches, entranced. He knocks back his Tequila. Nan pours him another drink.

NAN: So – you any good in the sack, Philip? (*Beat, clarifying*) Between the sheets. Do you do produce the goods? (*Winks*)

PHIL: I've not... I/mean...

NAN: You better sort yourself out, son. A young girl like that don't want a wet week in Margate.

PHIL: Oh, no/I'm not...

NAN: No's right. What she needs is a proper man who'll get her juices flowing. (*Laughs, nudges him* *knowingly*)

PHIL: I think you've... I mean/I haven't...

NAN: (*peers at him more closely*) Do you?

PHIL: Mm?

NAN: Get her juices flowing?

PHIL: I don't think so.

NAN: (*confidentially*) You want something for it?

Phil hesitates. He glances towards Julie who is still dancing.

PHIL: I.../no thanks...

NAN: Or are you more into the natural remedies?

PHIL: Sorry?

NAN: 'Cos a well-placed punnet of strawberries'll have your fighter sperm punching above their weight in no time. (*Winks confidentially*) Fact.

PHIL: I.../er...

NAN: (*gravely*) Well, it's your funeral.

PHIL: I hope not. (*Laughs nervously*)

Nan does not laugh. Beat.

JULIE: (*calls*) What are you two gossiping about?

PHIL: (*calls*) My funeral.

JULIE: (*calls*) My what?

PHIL: (*calls*) Don't worry about it.

Julie shrugs and continues to dance. Phil watches her, sipping his drink. Nan watches Phil. There is a knock at the door, breaking the spell.

NAN: Who the hell's that?

JULIE: (*turning down the music*) Shall I..?

NAN: Nah, I'll go. You stay here with your fancy man. (*Going to the door*)

PHIL: Honestly, I'm not/her...

NAN: (*kissing Julie's forehead*) You're an angel. (*To Phil*) She's an angel this one. (*Opens* the *door. To the* *person outside, aggressively*) What the fuck do you want?

Nan steps out, closing the door behind her. Occasionally we hear her raised voice. Phil coughs, laughs nervously.

PHIL: I think your Nan's got the wrong end of the stick.

JULIE: Has she?

PHIL: Of course. I'm not here to... Not that I... I mean... You're very attractive...

JULIE: I'm fucking with you.

PHIL: (*relieved*) Oh... right...

NAN: (*offstage, shouts*) A hundred grand! You're having a laugh.

JULIE: I'd ask for more money if I were you - she's in a good mood today.

NAN: (*offstage, shouting*) Don't you dis me, you smart arse, or I'll get Geoff to break both your legs.

Phil knocks back the rest of his drink and pours himself another.

NAN: (*offstage*) Now are we done? 'Cos I've got guests and there's nothing I hate more than rudeness. (*Enters, slamming the door behind her*) Cunt!

Beat.

JULIE: (*to Phil*) Go on.

Phil shakes his head frantically. He looks demented.

NAN: What's wrong with him?

JULIE: He wants a loan.

NAN: (*scrutinising him*) Does he indeed?

Nan scrutinises him for a while. Phil shifts nervously, coughs.

NAN: How much you looking for?

PHIL: I'm not... I mean... Only if/you...

NAN: Come on, son, spit it out. I haven't got all day.

PHIL: No... Of course...

NAN: (*to Julie*) Is he special needs or something?

JULIE: (*to Phil*) Tell Nan how much you'd like to borrow.

PHIL: (*tentatively*) Twenty grand.

NAN: Twenty, ey?

Phil glances at Julie who gestures for him to go for a larger amount.

PHIL: Though I could really do with forty five...

NAN: I see...

PHIL: Only if you can spare it.

NAN: Oh, I can spare it, dickhead. The question is can you pay it back.

PHIL: I assure you/I...

NAN: Words, son – they don't mean shit. What can you give me for collateral?

PHIL: Collateral?

NAN: You know, jewellery, benefit books, deeds of your house. Lamborghini. Fine Art collection.

Julie nods encouragement and Phil gets the plastic bag of jewellery. Nan holds out her hand. Phil hesitates, then hands it over.

PHIL: You will keep them safe?

NAN: Oh, I'll look after them as if they were my own. (*Fixes the eyeglass in her eye and opens a jewellery box – it contains a silver and turquoise necklace*)

PHIL: Only Linda doesn't know I've taken them.

NAN: (*looks at him sharply*) Linda?

JULIE: His wife.

NAN: I see...

Nan examines each piece of jewellery carefully with the eye glass. Phil watches nervously.

NAN: Mmm... Some nice pieces here... (*Examining the last piece*) I can give you... five on these.

PHIL: Five?

NAN: Go on then, six. I'm in a good mood. (*To Julie*) He strikes a hard bargain, dunnee. (*Laughs, then to Phil*) So - what else you got? (*She opens her notebook* *and pulls out a pencil in anticipation, making notes on the answers to her questions)*

PHIL: Nothing.

NAN: No house?

PHIL: It's in Linda's name.

NAN: She insured?

PHIL: Yes...

NAN: You sole beneficiary?

PHIL: (*hesitates*) Yes.

Beat.

NAN: I think we can come to some arrangement. (*Turns away*) Now... where did I put my..? (*Goes round the room picking up things and shaking them – a tin, a jar - dismissing each in turn*) No... no... no... (*Picks up the skull and peers inside, angrily exclaiming*) Fuckin' hell! (*To Phil*) There used to be a ton in there. (*Exits to the kitchen*)

There is a quantity of banging offstage. ***Phil*** *looks terrified.*

NAN: (*offstage*) Christ on a bike!

Loud crash. Silence.

PHIL: (*calls*) Are you OK?

Beat.

JULIE: (*calls*) Nan?

Beat.

NAN: (*enters dishevelled with a frozen turkey in one hand and a hatchet in the other*) Fucking fridge. (*Sticks her hand inside the turkey and pulls out a wodge of notes*) How much you looking for again? (*Puts the turkey and hatchet on the table*)

PHIL: (*stunned*) Forty five.

Nan indicates to Phil – he holds out his hand automatically. She counts the notes into his hand under the following – they are all well-worn fifties.

PHIL: Is that a duck?

NAN: (*stops counting*) It's a frozen turkey. (*Resumes counting*)

JULIE: (*to Nan*) He's got a thing about ducks.

PHIL: (*defensively*) No I haven't

NAN: (*placing the last note in his hand*) There - forty five thousand. Don't spend it all at once.

Phil laughs nervously.

NAN: (*gripping his wrist before he can take the money*) Now listen son, we have rules. (*She takes a document from the top of a pile of papers*) I'm friendly but firm, if you know what I mean.

PHIL: (*nodding eagerly*) Right.

NAN: Once we've worked out a monthly payment plan, you stick to it. Then we'll stay friends.

PHIL: (*nodding eagerly*) Right.

NAN: 'Cos I don't want be sitting here on me tod come payment day looking like a nun's chuff.

PHIL: (*nods, slightly bemused*) Right.

NAN: (*to Julie*) Jesus! He's like that nodding dog on the telly. (*To Phil*) I hope you're more exciting than this in bed.

***Julie** laughs. **Phil** laughs nervously.*

NAN: You miss a payment, the interest's a hundred per cent. You miss two, we break all your fingers. (*beat*) I'm only fucking with you. (*laughs*) Now go and screw my Granddaughter's brains out – she looks like she could do with a laugh.

PHIL: Oh, no/I don't...

NAN: (*to Julie*) And make sure he signs this – (*gravely*) in blood. (*Puts the document on the table and turns to go. She stops and turns back to Phil*) Oh - and I wouldn't hold onto them bank notes for too long if I were you.

PHIL: Why, are they... You know..? (*Winks knowingly*)

NAN: Are they what?

PHIL: Nicked.

NAN: Don't be a dick. They've been up a turkey's backside since Christmas. And, believe me, you don't wanna mess with Salmonella. (*Exits*)

Beat.

JULIE: Congratulations. (*Refills their glasses*)

PHIL: Thanks.

*Julie salts her hand, then hands Phil the lo salt. **Phil** salts his hand. They slam the Tequilas, leaving them breathless. They laugh. **Phil** lifts Julie's hair out of her eyes. Beat. They kiss. She wipes her mouth.*

PHIL: (*ironically*) Cheers. (*As in 'thanks'*)

JULIE: I don't want to catch your cold.

PHIL: Yeah - that'll make all the difference.

JULIE: (*going to the table and picking up the document*) Now I have to read you this.

***Phil** moves towards Julie. During the following **Phil** attempts to seduce Julie, kissing and undressing her, while **Julie** continues to read out the pact. There is a magical power to the words – as if he will be bound by them as long as she reads them out correctly.*

JULIE: (*avoids him, playfully*) You'll regret it if you don't listen.

PHIL: Go on then. (*Steps away, pouring himself another Tequila*)

JULIE: (*reading*) 'That the Lender' – that's my Nan – 'will pay to the Borrower' – that's you - the sum of forty five thousand pounds, inter alia.' (*She smiles, then reads on*) 'And in consideration of such payment, the Lender shall grant to the Borrower certain graces and favours/at the hands of...'

PHIL: (*puts his arms around her*) I like the sound of that/...

JULIE: (*reading*) 'That the existence of this pact shall remain a secret and the Borrower shall, de facto, be prohibited from making any reference to either the Lender or the grantor of favours' – that's my Nan and me.

PHIL: Definitely... (*He kisses her*)

JULIE: (*she shrugs off his kiss*) 'Ergo' (*reading*) 'the Borrower's obligations to repay the loan are set out pro rata in the Schedule appended to this pact.' (*Smiles and waves the paper*) 'Time shall be of the essence in relation to these repayments, and the Borrower hereby acknowledges that pacta sunt servandi. Therefore delay of any duration whatsoever and for any reason - be it man-made or by force of nature or act of...'

Phil *starts to undo Julie's top.* **Julie** *loses her place.*

JULIE: Sorry... (*She removes his hand, then resumes reading*) 'Be it deliberate or accidental - however bona fide - will permit the Lender to enforce her rights ad quod damnum under this pact in full and without further notice to the Borrower' - do you want to have a look at the schedule? (*Holds out contract*)

PHIL: (*fumbling inside Julie's clothing and kissing her*) Not right now.

JULIE: (*reading*) 'Upon the occurrence of any event of default on the part of the Borrower, the interest rate applicable under this pact, condicio sine qua non, shall immediately increase by four hundred per cent. Ad vitare dubium, all interest rates shall be calculated on a compound basis...'

PHIL: (*kissing her neck, continues to undo her top*) Yeah...

JULIE: (*trying to read the document*) 'Should any default continue beyond the Sabbath following the first full moon following that event of default' – that's the Sunday after the next... well, you know what a full moon is, innit. (*Laughs*)

***Phil** does not look up from kissing Julie, but mumbles agreement.*

JULIE: 'All of the Borrower's worldly goods and chattels shall immediately be forfeit to the Lender, peine forte et dure. (*She waits for a response*)

***Phil** continues to kiss her neck.*

JULIE: Are you paying attention?

PHIL: I'm hanging on your every word.

JULIE: Good, 'cos ignorantia juris non excusat — and this bit's important. (*Beat, reading*) 'That the Lender may employ any means whatsoever in terrorem in the enforcement of her rights under this pact, and the Borrower absolutely and irrevocably consents to any degree of coercion the Lender may deem fitting - cuius est solum eius est usque ad coelum et ad inferos...'

PHIL: (*passionately*) Oh... yes..!

JULIE: Listen! I don't want you coming back and saying...

PHIL: (*puts his hand inside her top*) And saying what?

JULIE: And saying that... (*Distracted*) that I've

misled you in any... in any... way...

PHIL: (*kisses her*) Yeah...

JULIE: (*kissing him*) Yeah...

Phil tries to take off Julie's top. ***Julie*** *stops him.*

JULIE: Wait – you've gotta sign this first or Nan'll go mad.

Julie *hands him the document then goes to the table and looks for a pen. She picks up the hatchet.*

PHIL: (*shocked*) Jesus!

JULIE: (*gravely*) Come on – let's get it over with.

PHIL: I... er... I don't/think I...

JULIE: (*laughs*) I'm fucking with you. (*She holds up a pen*)

PHIL: Oh...

Phil *takes the pen with relief, then hesitates, looks at Julie.* ***Julie*** *smiles at him.* ***Phil*** *signs.*

JULIE: Consummatum est. (*Smiles, takes pen and*

pact and puts them to one side) See, that didn't hurt, did it. (*Kisses him*)

*They kiss and start to undress. **Julie** mumbles rapidly throughout the following like an incantation, gradually growing louder as they become more passionate.*

JULIE: Libera me de morte æterna, in die illa tremenda: quando cœli movendi sunt et terra. Dum veneris iudicare sæculum per ignem.

PHIL: (*absently*) What?

JULIE: Tremens factus sum ego, et timeo, dum discussio venerit, atque ventura ira. Quando cœli movendi sunt et terra.

PHIL: God, that's sexy...

JULIE: (*more loudly*) Dies illa, dies iræ, calamitatis et miseriæ, dies magna et amara valde. Dum veneris iudicare sæculum per ignem.

PHIL: (*passionately*) Oh, yes.

JULIE: Requiem æternam dona eis...

PHIL: Yes!

The lights start to fade, as the chorus of 'Poker Face' fades up over:

JULIE: Et lux perpetua luceat eis. Libera me...

'Poker Face' continues to play. In the darkness the light up devils and skulls change colour from red to blue to green.

ACT 2

Nan sits in the rocking chair. She talks directly to the audience.

NAN: Once upon a time there was a beautiful baby – one of them prizewinning ones you see on the adverts. And it was in a pram outside a shop – Morrisons, I think – 'though the shop's not key. Could have been Tesco Metro for all I know. And a woman walks past who has no kids. 'Barren' she is - as they used to call them. And this barren woman she looks into the pram and she sees a little angel sitting there. Blue dungarees. Red t-shirt. No hair. Clutching a teddy in its hand. And as she looks, it sort of gives her the wink. (*Winks knowingly in imitation*) So the woman goes (*in a cooing to a baby voice*) 'What's a lovely lad like you doing outside Morrisons?' Or Tesco Metro or wherever it was. (*Cooing voice*) 'What's a lovely little lad doing out here alone?' But the baby doesn't answer - 'cos it's a baby and this isn't a fuckin' fairy tale. (*Laughs*) Then the barren woman has one of those moments – she gazes at the child and she thinks 'that could be mine'. (*Beat, she looks significantly at the audience*) And doubtless the mother ran out afterwards screaming blue murder and tearing her hair. But the baby didn't hear her 'cos she was far away. And when the barren woman got home she noticed it wasn't a boy – which happened pretty fast if truth be told, as she'd been with a few fellas in her time and knew a cock when she saw one. (*Laughs*) And she thought it was a bit rich to pretend she was her mum – given that she'd nicked her off the steps of Morrisons. So she told the kid she was her Nan. And she named her Julie. After Julie Andrews. And I was grumpy for a bit 'cos I'd set me heart on a lad – you know, for protection later on. But she grew up clever – and pretty too. So I don't regret it - not one bit. 'Cos my little stolen angel she goes nicking stuff for me. And every now and then she brings me a man. (*Laughs to herself*)

Jessie Jay's 'Price Tag' plays, cash registers ching, supermarket scanners, etc, as lights go down on Nan and up on:

SCENE 1

Phil and Linda's dining room. Seven months later. There has been a refurb. Old furniture has been replaced by a shiny new glass table and matching chrome chairs. The set of shelves now only contains one plant - Morris. On it instead are photos of Linda and Phil visiting Sydney Opera House, The Eiffel Tower, and

Disneyland. There are also several gadgets, a state of the art cordless phone and a TV remote control. Marks and Spencer and John Lewis bags are strewn about on the floor, together with an open punnet of Marks and Spencer strawberries. **Phil** *and* **Linda** *are wearing new clothes and no shoes - the only familiar item is Phil's jeans, shoplifted with Julie.* **Phil** *pops a champagne cork and pours two glasses. They laugh.*

LINDA: (*raising her glass*) To your promotion!

PHIL: (*raising his glass*) To the future!

LINDA/PHIL: (*together*) The future!

They drink.

LINDA: Ooh, this is lovely. (*Drinks, laughs*) The bubbles go right up your nose.

PHIL: Nothing's too good for my princess. (*He dips a strawberry in champagne and feeds it to her*)

LINDA: (*eating the strawberry*) Mmm... (*Leans back in the chair and drinks*) I'm ready for bed, are you?

PHIL: (*eating a strawberry sexily, nonchalantly crosses his legs*) I could be persuaded.

*They laugh and sip champagne. **Phil** realises his turn ups are caught on the side of the chair and tries to untangle himself.*

PHIL: (*under his breath*) Shit!

LINDA: (*laughs*) I wish you wouldn't wear those jeans.

PHIL: They're designer.

LINDA: Yeah - designed for a clown. (*Laughs*) Whoever sold you those saw you coming.

***Phil** tries to laugh. Pause. **Phil** looks mournfully at his jeans while **Linda** drinks her champagne and eats another strawberry.*

LINDA: Was everything all right with your card in the end?

PHIL: Mmm? (*Beat*) Oh, it was just some mix up with the accounts.

LINDA: Well, as long as they apologised. (*Takes a sip of her drink*)

Pause.

PHIL: (*looking at his jeans*) They're all right aren't they? The jeans?

LINDA: Fine - if you're planning to run away with the Circus/Did... (*Laughs*)

PHIL: (*laughing*) OK, OK/...

LINDA: Did they not have the wigs to/match?

PHIL: OK, you've made your point.

They laugh, feed each other strawberries and kiss.

PHIL: (*remembering*) I've got something for you.

LINDA: Is it a trapeze?

PHIL: Well, if you don't want it...

LINDA: No, I think I'd look very good upside down in a bikini.

PHIL: I think you would too. (*Kisses her, exits*)

Rustling from the hallway. Linda dips a strawberry in her champagne and eats it.

LINDA: (*calls*) What are you doing? (*Beat*) Phil?

PHIL: (*calls*) Hang on a minute.

More rustling. Silence. Phil's leg appears from behind the door – followed by Phil. He is wearing socks and boxers under a long fur coat and is humming 'Poker Face', singing 'I poke your face' at appropriate moments, poking his fingers towards Linda's face, kicking his legs around and posing in a very bad Lady Gaga imitation.

LINDA: Oh, Phil that's gorgeous..!

PHIL: And the coat?

***Linda** laughs. **Phil** does a couple more mock Gaga moves, finally removing the coat, and on an appropriate poke of Linda's face putting it around her shoulders. **Linda** starts to cry.*

PHIL: Don't you like it?

LINDA: No, it's not... (*Moved, strokes the coat*) It's... I love it. (*Kisses him, then jokily*) You're not having an affair are you! (*Laughs*)

PHIL: (*laughs*) Chance'd be a fine thing.

They kiss.

LINDA: You don't appear to have any trousers on.

PHIL: You said you didn't like them.

They laugh and kiss more passionately. Phil's mobile rings from the hallway. **Phil** *ignores it.*

LINDA: (*pulling away*) You better get that.

PHIL: I'll call them back. (*He kisses her*)

LINDA: (*pulling away*) You can't let anything slide now – you're an assistant general manager.

Phil *goes to kiss her.* **Linda** *resists.*

PHIL: All right – slave driver. (*Reluctantly stops kissing her*) Keep this warm for me. (*Gropes her, then hums the riff of 'Poker Face' making poking movements as he exits*)

Linda *laughs. (Offstage) In the hallway* **Phil** *answers the phone without looking at the caller's number. During the call* **Linda** *sails round the room in a fur-coat-filled blissful dream world, sipping champagne, eating strawberries, unpacking John Lewis bags of Emma Bridgewater crockery, shop-wrapped in tissue paper, admiring her purchases, and placing them on display on* *the shelves. We occasionally glimpse **Phil** on his mobile through the open door.*

PHIL: (*offstage, answering the phone*) Hello - Phil Haven. (*Whispers*) I told you not to... (*Beat*) I haven't, it's just... (*Beat*) I've no money at the moment. (*Beat*) I'm not lying. (*Laughs, nervously*) You're not serious. (*Stops laughing, beat*) No, no... don't - I'll get it for you. (*Beat*) Wait – Julie! (*She has hung up*) Julie?

*We see **Phil** (offstage) through the doorway, visibly shaken, sink to the floor, clutching the phone like a cornered animal. (Onstage) **Linda** stands back to admire her new crockery. She strokes her fur coat with satisfaction.*

LINDA: (*calls*) Is everything all right? (*Beat*) Phil?

PHIL: (*calls*) Fine.

Beat.

LINDA: (*seductively arranging herself in the fur coat on the carpet, and strategically placing some strawberries on herself, calls*) Phil?

PHIL: (*calls*) Yes?

LINDA: (*calls*) Aren't you going to come back in and finish your champagne?

INTERLUDE 1

In the darkness an instrumental of 'Poker Face' by the Vitamin String Quartet plays.

SCENE 2

Phil and Linda's dining room. The next day. The Emma Bridgewater crockery is proudly on display on the shelves, as is Morris. Offstage someone is trying to shut the door – it still sticks.

LINDA: (*offstage*) You have to give it a good shove or it won't shut.

Offstage, door bangs loudly.

LINDA: If you wouldn't mind, we've a no shoe policy (*laughs apologetically*) – new carpet, you see. And cream marks quite badly.

(Offstage) **Linda** *and* **Julie** *take their shoes off.* **Linda**

enters, carrying shopping bags and a jewellery box – the sort that would contain a chunky necklace – which she puts on the table. We have seen this box before – it contains one of the pieces of jewellery Nan examined. The jewellery box should not be immediately obvious to the audience. There is a sense throughout this scene that **Linda** *is bewitched by* **Julie**.

LINDA: (*calls*) Sorry to be a pain. Come in.

JULIE: (*enters – she is heavily pregnant*) This is kind of you.

LINDA: (*putting bags down*) Not at all. You've done me a big favour. Here – (*moving a bag, indicates chair*)

JULIE: Thanks. (*Sits*)

LINDA: I really am very grateful.

JULIE: Anyone would have done the same.

LINDA: I doubt that. You should see some of the tearaways that hang about round here. It's a good job you're so honest. (*Laughs*)

Beat.

LINDA: When are you due?

JULIE: (*rubbing her bump*) Six weeks.

LINDA: You must be excited.

JULIE: Over the moon.

*Beat. **Linda** stares admiringly at Julie's bump.*

LINDA: Can I..? (*Holding her hand towards the bump*)

JULIE: I'd rather you didn't.

LINDA: Of course. (*She withdraws her hand*)

JULIE: Sorry to be... you know... fussy. (*Laughs*)

LINDA: It's a mother's prerogative isn't it? (*Laughs*)

Beat.

LINDA: I'm Linda by the way.

JULIE: Julie.

LINDA: Well, it was my lucky day, Julie, when I bumped into you.

***Linda** smiles, then unpacks the bags. **Julie** looks at the photos: Linda and Phil in Paris by the Eiffel Tower;*

Linda and Phil in Disneyland; Linda and Phil in front of Sidney Opera House.

JULIE: You've a lovely house.

LINDA: Thanks.

JULIE: (*examining an Emma Bridgewater cup*) I've always wanted a set of these.

LINDA: Me too.

JULIE: There's something classy about it isn't there.

LINDA: I think so.

JULIE: To have all your cups totally fucking clashing.

LINDA: We haven't had them long. (*Takes the cup from her*)

JULIE: Ooh! (*Picking up Morris*) Who's this then?

LINDA: Oh, that's Morris.

JULIE: Morris?

LINDA: I know, silly really.

JULIE: (*to the plant, with a seraphic smile*) Hello, Morris.

LINDA: I used to have loads, but you can't really keep them, can you, when you travel a lot.

JULIE: Well, you held onto the best one.

LINDA: (*like a proud mother*) I think so.

JULIE: (*peers closely at the plant*) You're a lovely boy, aren't you, Morris. (*Flicks a leaf playfully – it falls off. Holding the leaf out*) Oh, sorry...

LINDA: Don't worry. He does that sometimes. Probably just needs a drink of water. (*To the plant*) Don't you, Morris. (*Reaches out her hand for the plant, but is distracted by:*)

Offstage, the front door opens, sticks then bangs shut. ***Phil*** *is whistling 'Happy Talk'.*

LINDA: That'll be Phil now. (*Calls*) Hello!

PHIL: (*offstage, calls*) Hello, love. (*He takes his shoes off in the hall and calls*) I've got something for you.

LINDA: (*calls*) Have you? (*To Julie*) He's always

buying me little presents.

Julie puts the plant down. As Linda turns to greet Phil, Julie points and hisses at the plant then laughs to herself, unseen by Linda. Phil enters carrying an enormous red heart-shaped box of chocolates. He stops abruptly when he sees Julie. Beat.

LINDA: This is Julie.

JULIE: Hi.

PHIL: Hi.

Beat.

LINDA: She found my necklace – you know the silver one with the turquoise that Mum gave me?

Phil stares at Julie.

LINDA: You'll never guess where it was.

PHIL: Surprise me.

LINDA: Only right outside our front door in the grass.

JULIE: It must have fallen off the window ledge.

LINDA: Isn't that amazing?

PHIL: Amazing.

LINDA: (*looking at the necklace*) We can't lay our hands on half our stuff these days, what with the building work and everything. They only put up the new shed yesterday, so I haven't had a chance to unpack the boxes. (*Laughs*) I hope nothing else has gone missing.

JULIE: Oh, I'm sure it hasn't.

Beat.

JULIE: We've already met.

PHIL: Have we?

LINDA: Oh, where?

JULIE: Don't you remember?

PHIL: No...

JULIE: In the park. You feed the ducks.

LINDA: He loves ducks. (*Laughs, beat*) What am I thinking! Tea?

JULIE: Oh, you don't have/to...

LINDA: Nonsense. It's the least I can do. (*Takes a box of tea out of one of the plastic bags*) Is Earl Grey all right?

JULIE: Lovely.

LINDA: We're a bit adhoc at the minute, I'm afraid, 'til they put the range in the new kitchen. You know how it is.

JULIE: Yeah.

LINDA: (*glancing at Morris*) You look like you could do with a drink too, young man. (*Laughs, picks up the pot plant. To Morris*) Come on.

Julie smiles at her. Linda goes out to make the tea, carrying Morris and the box of Earl Grey. We occasionally hear noises from the kitchen during their hushed exchange. There is a demonic edge to Julie's levity throughout the following:

JULIE: Your cough's better.

PHIL: What do you want, Julie?

JULIE: You don't call, you don't visit, you don't even

go to the park no more. (*Pouts ostentatiously*) The ducks miss you.

PHIL: I've already told you, I've no money.

JULIE: Don't feel you can take advantage of my better nature just 'cos we/you know...

PHIL: I'm not.

JULIE: Good. 'Cos you got obligations – that's obligatio as in binding, not obliviscor as in to completely fucking forget.

Beat.

PHIL: Is it..? (*Nodding towards her stomach*)

JULIE: What?

PHIL: Is it mine?

JULIE: You give anything to Oxfam recently?

PHIL: (*puzzled*) No.

JULIE: Then I doubt it. (*Lifts up her jumper to reveal a flowery cushion*) Everyone trusts a pregnant lady. (*Laughs*) Was you worried?

Beat.

JULIE: Did you think we'd be getting together to pick baby names? I like Ikea for a girl. (*Picks up the box of chocolates*) Lovely chocolates by the way. Nice gesture. (*Examining the box, looks at the types of chocolates on the back, then opens the box, chooses one and eats it*) Mmm... They haven't skimped on the cocoa, haven't they? (*Stops chewing momentarily*) Funny word that, innit – skimped. Wonder where it comes from. (*Resumes chewing*) Probably Norse. They were whores for the letter k.

Phil *tries to take the box from her, but stops in his tracks when he hears Linda's voice.*

LINDA: (*offstage, calls*) Do you take milk, Julie?

JULIE: (*calls*) Please.

LINDA: (*offstage, calls*) Sugar?

JULIE: (*calls*) No, thanks. I'm sweet enough. (*Smiles sweetly at Phil, then looks around her*) Where d'you tell her all this money come from?

PHIL: I said I'd got a promotion.

Phil rests his head in his hands.

JULIE: (*with mock sympathy*) Ah, is this not the happy ending you was hoping for? (*Eats another chocolate, gags, takes it out of her mouth and looks at it in disgust*) I hate that, don't you, when they disguise a nut as a soft centre? (*Lifts the lid of the Emma Bridgwater teapot and drops the half eaten chocolate inside, shuddering and wiping her hands on her top*) Eugh!

Phil tries to wrestle the chocolates from her just as Linda pops her head into the room.

LINDA: Would you like some biscuits?

Phil and Julie stop fighting. Phil is left panting, clutching the heart-shaped box.

JULIE: (*as if nothing has happened*) Yes, please.

LINDA: (*lightly*) Whatever's going on here?

PHIL: I'm...

JULIE: He's just showing me his Kung Fu moves. Aren't you, Philip? (*Gestures, accompanied by an appropriate Kung Fu sound*)

LINDA: Kung Fu?

Julie does a Karate chop.

LINDA: (*laughs*) Well, just be careful near the new crockery. (*Returns to the kitchen*)

Pause.

JULIE: She's lovely, in't she.

PHIL: I think so.

JULIE: Kill her. (*She points at the kitchen door, hisses*)

Phil laughs. Julie does not laugh. Phil stops laughing.

PHIL: You're serious.

JULIE: Nan wants her money back.

PHIL: If she could just wait/a little (longer)...

JULIE: I think she's been more than patient, don't you? Besides, she fancies a new freezer. And they've a special offer down Comet that ends Tuesday.

PHIL: It... It could be a bit tricky/you see...

JULIE: She thought you might say that, so she give me a message to pass on –

PHIL: But/I've not...

JULIE: Hang on – I have to get this right or there'll be hell to pay. (*Laughs edgily*) Oh, yeah - (*self-consciously remembering*) 'she's very sorry but a deal's a deal, and if you don't cough up for the last three months you've missed... she's going to ask Geoff to break all your fingers.' (*Smiles and wiggles her fingers at him*)

Beat.

PHIL: Who's Geoff?

JULIE: He lives next door. Does odd jobs for us.

Beat.

JULIE: Sorry. Nan can be a bit strict. Especially about interest.

PHIL: Interest?

JULIE: It's four hundred per cent at this stage.

***Phil** puts his head in his hands in despair.*

JULIE: Ah, don't be a moody sourpuss. She's insured, in't she? 'Linda.'

PHIL: Yes/but...

JULIE: Listen, mate, we all have to do things in this life we don't enjoy. Look at me with you. That weren't no walk in the park.

PHIL: I/thought...

JULIE: You didn't think I loved you did you? (*Laughs*) Oh, come on, cheer up. If you can't stand the heat don't build a patio.

Phil stares at Julie.

JULIE: I can't see what your problem is. Stab her, poison her, kick the bitch's brains in. Make it look like a bodged burglary. Be imaginative - and for fuck's sake do it soon - 'cos Comet don't have them special offers all year round.

Beat.

Linda enters with a tea tray. The cups are in different designs of Emma Bridgewater. There is also a plate of 'homemade' shop bought biscuits. Julie hastily covers her belly/cushion with her top.

LINDA: (*entering, cheerily*) Here we go. (*Puts tray on* *table, then hands Julie a cup)*

JULIE: (*taking cup*) Thanks.

Linda *tries to hand Phil a cup, but he is holding the heart-shaped box of chocolates. They laugh nervously and swap, leaving* ***Linda*** *with the box of chocolates and* ***Phil*** *the tea in an Emma Bridgwater 'men at work' mug.*

LINDA: These look lovely.

Linda *kisses him and puts the chocolates on the table. Pause while they drink their tea.*

JULIE: She's very kind, your wife. I hope you cherish her.

LINDA: Oh, he does.

Linda *offers Phil and Julie the plate containing long, finger-shaped biscuits.* ***Phil*** *declines.* ***Julie*** *takes several. Then meaningfully snaps a biscuit in two.* ***Phil*** *flinches.*

LINDA: (*to Phil*) Are you OK?

PHIL: Fine.

LINDA: You've gone very pale.

JULIE: (*eating*) These are lovely biscuits.

LINDA: Aren't they.

JULIE: Do you make them yourself?

LINDA: No. (*Laughs*) I bought them in the bakery on the corner. They're a bit more expensive but we think they're worth it – don't we?

PHIL: Yes.

Pause - they drink their tea.

LINDA: (*pulls a face*) Does this tea taste odd to you?

JULIE: It's meant to be like flowers, innit.

LINDA: (*sniffs the cup*) The milk's not gone sour?

PHIL: It's fine, love, really.

There is an awkward pause. ***Julie*** *munches her biscuit loudly.* ***Linda*** *smiles politely.*

LINDA: Phil's a managing director.

PHIL: That's not/strictly (true)...

JULIE: Is he?

PHIL: I'm Assistant General Manager.

LINDA: He's recently been promoted.

JULIE: Clever Phil.

Julie snaps another biscuit in two. Phil winces.

LINDA: (*to Phil*) What's the matter?

PHIL: I... (*He looks at Julie, beat*) Nothing.

LINDA: Well, cheer up then. It might never happen. (*Laughs*)

JULIE: (*eating ravenously*) Anyway, if it did 'happen' I'm sure you two'd be well covered.

LINDA: What do you mean?

JULIE: Insurance and that. Your Phil looks like the type who'd have it all sorted. (*She smiles at Phil, then at Linda*) 'Ensurance' - did you know they used it of lovers, back in the day?

LINDA: No, I didn't. That's very interesting. Isn't it interesting, Phil?

JULIE: Like when you got betrothed you gave your word – 'thereto I plight my troth'/

LINDA: (*recognising the phrase, enthusiastically*) Oh/yes...

JULIE: And once you'd given your word you couldn't renege, 'cos it was like a solemn binding promise on peril of your soul – (*tasting the word*) 'ensurance'.

LINDA: Really?

JULIE: (*nods, chewing*) Mmm - they were quite big on it.

LINDA: I suppose it's just being practical, isn't it. I mean, nobody lives for ever.

JULIE: They certainly don't – do they, Philip? (*Snaps biscuit*)

PHIL: (*quietly*) No. They don't.

Beat. ***Julie*** *reaches for the plate, but all the biscuits are gone.*

LINDA: (*apologetically*) Oh, have all the biscuits gone?

JULIE: Sorry, I'm eating for two.

LINDA: No need to apologise. You need to keep your strength up – doesn't she, Phil?

Julie wiggles her fingers at Phil.

PHIL: Yeah.

Linda exits to the kitchen with the empty plate. Phil sits with his head in his hands. Julie smiles and picks the crumbs off her bump and eats them. (Offstage) Linda lets out an ear-piercing scream. Phil leaps to his feet. Julie continues to pick crumbs off her bump, barely raising her head.

PHIL: Linda? (*Beat*) Linda, are you all right?

Beat. Linda enters in tears, cradling a withered pot plant.

LINDA: (*holding out the pot plant*) It's Morris. He's dead.

Phil tries to comfort her.

LINDA: (*pushing him away, gags*) Oh... (*Puts her hand to her mouth*) I feel sick... (*Runs out*)

PHIL: (*calls after her*) Linda..! (*Exits, then offstage, calls*) Linda – are you all right?

***Julie** remains seated, smiling and eating biscuit crumbs off her bump.*

Interlude 3

In the darkness as voiceover - a series of TV advertisements, accompanied by the appropriate music:

VO1: Sometimes we don't like to think about our own funeral or that of a loved one...

The TV channel is changed.

VO2: Are you finding your home insurance a little pricey? We've got the ideal solution for you...

A female opera singer sings a ridiculous insurance based jingle. The TV channel is hastily changed.

VO3: (*accompanied by jaunty music*) Comet Sale! Fabulous offers on washing machines, dishwashers, fridges <u>and</u> freezers! (*Rapidly*) Terms and conditions apply - must end Tuesday! (*Jaunty music swells*)

The TV is switched off.

SCENE 3

Phil stands alone in the light.

PHIL: The Comet Sale ends Tuesday – oh my God! It's Sunday now!

Phil rifles through his pockets, frantically pulling out small change, tissues, a shoe lace. He gets out his wallet and counts out fifteen pounds and then the change.

PHIL: Fifteen pounds and sixty pence - (*throws money on ground*) it's not enough!
(*Has an idea – frantically takes his credit cards out of his wallet*)
I could get more credit on my cards, maybe... (*Throws cards on floor in despair*)
Who am I kidding? I couldn't even put
My shopping on them when we last went out.
(*With a bitter smile through clenched teeth*)
'Computer says no, we're very sorry, sir –
May we suggest you kill your wife instead?' (*Crying, head in hands*)
I wish I hadn't met that little bitch.
I wish I hadn't taken out a loan.
I wish the Comet sale would never end! (*Sobs*)

His mobile rings. He goes to answer it – looks at the

display.

PHIL: Oh, God, it's her! (*Hesitates, then accepts the call, tentatively*) Hi, Julie. (*Beat*) No,
I haven't, but... I understand that... Geoff!
Tell him he doesn't need to... Outside now? (*Looks around him, terrified*)
Look, I'll find the money somehow, just don't...
No, please... let me explain... (*In tears*) Please, Julie – no!

Phil hangs up, sobbing. His mobile rings again. He looks at it, terrified, lets it ring. It stops. It starts to ring again. He puts a cushion on top of it. He stares at the cushion. Beat. The phone stops. He sits sobbing, reaches out in the darkness for a tissue – finds Aloe Vera hand cream, Marks and Spencer stomach support tights, the heart-shaped box of chocolates.

PHIL: What's the point of all this useless shit?
(*Throws them on floor in disgust*).
(*In another world*) Better to give up, and declare yourself
Bankrupt. I've seen them on the telly - bankrupts.
They look light as air. They can't be touched.
A bankrupt's blank. They're nothing. Nobody.
They...

*There is a knock at the door. **Phil** freezes, then gets down on all fours and crawls towards the door. There is a slant of light as the enormous letter box opens, we see Julie's eyes peering in, then the letterbox snaps shut on Julie's fingers.*

JULIE: (*in pain*) Fuck!

***Phil** hardly dares to breathe. The letter box opens. We see Julie's eyes. **Julie** becomes increasingly more demonic during the scene.*

Pause.

***Phil** pretends to be invisible by being a statue.*

JULIE: I <u>can</u> see you, you know, you stupid twat.

***Phil** flinches.*

JULIE: (*laughs*) Did you flinch then? It's just a word - 'twat' - it can't hurt you. The word's Old Norse – though the concept's timeless.

PHIL: Go away!

JULIE: Not possible, I'm afraid. Geoff's with me, see. He'd like a chat.

PHIL: (*under his breath*) Shit!

Beat.

JULIE: If you was to research the history of swearing - you'd see there's been quite a societal shift towards the scatological, and away from traditional religious profanity, such as 'oh God', or 'bloody', or 'gadzoons'. (*Shouts*) Gadzoons! (*Laughs maniacally*)

PHIL: (*desperately*) Leave me alone!

JULIE: I nearly pissed myself laughing when I first heard that. Gadzoons! You wanna branch out, mate, 'cos it's a lot better than the usual shit. (*Laughs*) Better than the usual shit, that's a good one that. (*Laughs*) Better than the usual shit... (*Laughs*) I crack myself up sometimes... (*Laughs*)

PHIL: Can't we/just..?

JULIE: (*whispers*) Gadzoons! See, that don't offend you, but if you was Medieval you'd be well pissed off by now.

PHIL: I need more time.

JULIE: Gadzoons! (*Beat, laughs*) Can you imagine

using that in a fight: 'Yo yo bro, I is so goin' ta mash y'up big stylie.' 'Gadzoons, bredren, I'd rather you didn't.' It'd solve all the strife in the World, wouldn't it – gadzoons? We'd all die laughing. (*Laughs maniacally*)

PHIL: (*crying*) Please, leave me alone... I haven't got any money.

JULIE: No rich relative or family heirlooms hidden away? No unwanted gold or jewellery?

PHIL: (*shouts*) No! (*Beat*) Wait. (*Takes off his watch*) How much would I get for this?

JULIE: What's it made of?

PHIL: It's an Accurist.

JULIE: That's not a metal it's a lifestyle choice. (*Beat*) We can do cash for silver, cash for bronze, cash for copper, cash for lead, cash for stainless steel – that's a popular one – you got any of that, I can give you a good price.

Beat.

Phil does not respond, but sits with his head in his

hands.

JULIE: (*resumes*) Cash for aluminium, cash for iron, cash for gold, cash for brass/cash for tin...

PHIL: (*looking up*) Cash for gold?

JULIE: Yeah. (*Beat, in a voice reminiscent of the ad*) Do you have any unwanted gold?

PHIL: (*looks at his wedding ring*) Yes, I do. It's my... I mean, it's not unwanted/but...

JULIE: Hand it over then. (*Shoves her hand through the letter box – it snaps shut on her*) Bastard!

***Phil** tries to get the ring off – it is too small. He licks his finger, removes it with effort – stares at it.*

PHIL: (*weighs the ring in his hand – it seems very light. He notices Julie is not there, calls*) Julie? (*Beat*) Are you still there? (*Beat – he tentatively opens the letter box*) Julie?

JULIE: It's lethal that letterbox. I could sue. (*Laughs edgily*) You're lucky I'm so good natured.

***Phil** holds the ring into the light from the letterbox. **Julie** peers at it. Beat.*

JULIE: I'll give you thirty quid for it.

*Pause. **Phil** stares at the ring.*

JULIE: (*calls*) Make a decision, mate – 'cos my back's breaking leaning through this fucking letter box. (*Letter box snaps shut - she shouts in frustration*) Gadzoons!

*The flap of the letter box flies across the room. **Phil** jumps. His wedding ring rolls onto the floor.*

PHIL: Shit!

***Julie** laughs, and continues to laugh as **Phil** crawls about the floor frantically looking for the ring. He finds a packet of seeds, the book 'A Hundred and One Things to do before you Die', the Aloe Vera hand cream, stomach support tights. Eventually he finds the ring, and sits clutching it, panting, like a cornered animal.*

JULIE: Come on, Philip, open up. It's freezing out here.

PHIL: It's not for sale.

***Phil** tries to put the ring back on his finger. It is even more difficult to get back on than it was to take off. He* *licks his finger – it won't go on.*

JULIE: (*with mock sympathy*) Ah – will it not fit you anymore?

PHIL: (*struggling with the ring*) Go away!

Phil *struggles with the ring.*

JULIE: Fingers gone a bit porky, have they?

PHIL: Leave me alone!

JULIE: That's middle age spread that is – it affects all your fleshy bits. (*Laughs dirtily*)

PHIL: (*shifts uncomfortably – he has been sitting on the Aloe Vera hand cream. Under his breath*) Hello, Vera. (*He has an idea – he opens the cream and rubs some on his finger, under his breath*) Come on, come on... (*Pushes the ring onto his finger – it still won't fit*) Don't let me down... (*Licks his finger – reacts to the taste of the cream*) Eugh!

JULIE: Tastes a bit sour, dunnit – regret. (*Laughs*)

Phil *ignores her and gives the ring one final heave - it goes back on.*

PHIL: (*laughs, relieved*) Ah! (*Reaches out his hand to show Julie*)

JULIE: I'm pleased for you. Now, open up. (*Bangs on the door*)

PHIL: (*clutching his wedding ring, calls*) Do what you like to me, I'm not going to kill her.

JULIE: Come on, Philip – (*bangs on the door, beat, then sweetly*) I only want a chat about rescheduling your payment plan.

PHIL: Really. (*Laughs to himself bitterly, glances at the ring, then goes to the door, resigned to his fate*) Come on then...

JULIE: 'Cos a little bird tells me you'll be needing more money. (*Laughs*)

PHIL: (*undoing the latch*) Let's get it over with...

JULIE: And Geoff here wants a word about your skiing accident.

PHIL: (*stops*) Skiing accident? (*Beat, calls*) What skiing accident? (*Beat*) Julie? (*Opens the door, curious, looks out*) Hello? (*Beat*) Julie?

JULIE: Welcome to fuckin' Val d'Isere.

*A fist punches **Phil** in the face – the front door slams shut – blackout.*

Interlude 2

In the darkness we hear the sound of Phil being beaten up - kicks, punches, groans and Julie's occasional laughter - and at the same time, someone flicking through TV channels. Bong – a kick and groan. As voiceover - news headlines -

VO1: Global recession continues as yet another country falls foul of the Eurozone Crisis.

Bong – a kick and groan. Channel changed by remote. As voiceover, a nature programme -

VO2: And after mating the female of the species unceremoniously eats her prey.

Kick and groan. Channel changed by remote. As voiceover, advertisement -

VO3: Come to Comet sale! Fabulous offers! Absolutely has to end - tomorrow!

Kick and groan. Channel changed by remote. As voiceover, continuity announcer -

VO4: And next, the ultimate heist for George Clooney and Brad Pitt - in 'Ocean's Eleven'!

The theme for 'Ocean's Eleven' plays and continues under the start of the following scene:

Scene 4

Dining Room and garden of Phil and Linda's House. The next day, evening. The theme tune of 'Ocean's Eleven' still plays under the following. **Phil** *enters the garden, dragging a wheelie bin in the semi-darkness. Occasionally he winces with pain from his beating. He has a pair of Linda's tights on his head, though not pulled down over his face, which is badly bruised.* **Linda** *is in the Dining Room. On the verge of tears, she clears up the debris from the previous scene.* **Phil** *hesitates, then calls Linda on his mobile. The phone rings. We see them both simultaneously – one inside, the other outside the house.* **Linda** *picks up the TV remote and lowers the volume.*

LINDA: *(answering the phone)* Hello?

PHIL: Hello, love.

LINDA: Are you on your way home?

PHIL: Sorry - they've... they've asked me to work late on the er... Maldon Contract.

LINDA: But we were meant to be meeting the others at eight.

PHIL: You'll have to go without me. Sorry.

LINDA: Ah, Phil - I didn't see you last night either.

PHIL: (*defensively*) You were asleep when I got in.

LINDA: You left a terrible mess.

PHIL: Did I?

LINDA: And the house smells funny.

PHIL: Sorry...

LINDA: And the flap's broken on the new letterbox.

PHIL: I noticed that too/...

LINDA: I had to bin it.

Beat.

PHIL: How are you feeling?

LINDA: I'm just tired.

PHIL: Right... Of course...

Beat.

LINDA: I buried him by the shed.

PHIL: He would have liked that.

LINDA: Do you think?

PHIL: Yeah.

Beat

LINDA: I better... you know – 'Oceans Eleven's' starting.

PHIL: Are you not going out then?

LINDA: No, I don't feel like it.

PHIL: Oh. (*Beat*) Well... have a lovely time with Brad.

LINDA: I will.

Beat.

PHIL: Linda?

LINDA: Yeah?

PHIL: I love you.

LINDA: I love you too. (*Hangs up*)

(Inside) **Linda** *picks up the remote and turns the TV volume up – theme for 'Ocean's Eleven' still plays. She throws the heart shaped chocolate box to one side and sits, wriggling uncomfortably, then watches the TV, cradling the empty flower pot that once contained Morris as if it was a dead baby. (Outside)* **Phil** *puts his mobile away, then pulls the tights over his face wincing with pain – they are stomach support tights so he can't see through them. He stumbles into the bin.*

PHIL: (*under his breath*) Shit! (*Takes the tights off his head and tries with difficulty to make eye holes in them with his nails*) Ow! (*Shakes his hand in pain, bangs* *into something else*) Ow! What the hell do they make these things out of – Kevlar?

Linda *hears the noise and looks out of the window. She sees the shadowy figure of a man –* ***Phil*** *– up to no good behind her wheelie bin.*

LINDA: (*to herself*) What's <u>he</u> doing?

Linda *puts the pot down carefully on the table, turns off the TV, then calls Phil's mobile. It rings.* ***Phil*** *frantically tries to find it. His fingers are trapped in the eye holes in the tights.* ***Linda*** *watches him through the window.*

PHIL: (*trying to find his phone and pull his fingers out of the tights*) Shit! Shit!

LINDA: (*under her breath*) Come on, Phil - answer the phone...

Phil *turns the phone off.* ***Linda*** *is simultaneously cut off. She watches the man stumbling about outside, hesitates, then calls the Police.*

LINDA: (*into phone, anxiously*) Yes. Police. There's someone trying to break into my house.

Phil falls against the wheelie bin, knocking it over. Rubbish pours everywhere — Marks and Spencer food packaging, an empty strawberry punnet, bottles, the broken flap of the letterbox, the empty heart-shaped box of chocolates.

PHIL: (*under his breath*) Shit! (*Shoves the tights back on his head, though not over his face, then tries to put the rubbish back in the bin*)

LINDA: (*peering out of the window, whispers into the phone*) He seems to be... tidying up the garden..? (*Puzzled*) Yes, it is strange... (*Beat*) That's OK, I'm not going anywhere. (*Hangs up*)

PHIL: (*noticing the pile of earth*) Sorry, Morris. (*Straightening the earth, he tries not to cry*)

LINDA: (*puts her hands to her breasts, winces*) Pff! I feel the size of a house today. (*Peers out of the window*) Is he..? He is - he's digging up Morris! (*Looking around for something to use as a weapon, with determination*) Right..!

Phil abandons the rubbish, picks up a brick, and using the bin climbs up onto the shed roof. He stumbles – there is a bang.

PHIL: Shit! (*He rubs his bruised ribs, winces*)

Linda picks up the Emma Bridgewater tea pot and assesses its weight. It rattles. She lifts the lid and looks inside.

LINDA: Ew! (*She tips up the teapot. Julie's half-chewed chocolate nut drops out. She gags*) Oh, disgusting! (*She puts the teapot down. Instead she picks up the flower pot and clasps it to herself for courage and exits the house*)

Phil hides as Linda, now outside, looks around.

LINDA: (*calls*) Who's there? (*Beat, with bravado*) I think I should warn you I'm armed.

Noticing the half-cleared rubbish Linda follows the trail and climbs up to the shed roof, using the wheelie bin to help her. It is not easy as she's carrying the pot. Bracing herself, she raises the pot above her head, peers over the edge of the roof, sees someone and screams. Phil drops the brick on his foot.

PHIL: (*hopping, in pain*) Shit! Shit!

Beat. Phil continues to hop about.

LINDA: Phil?

PHIL: Jesus, Lind!

LINDA: What are you doing up here?

PHIL: You scared me half to death.

Phil wiggles his foot to relieve the pain – the tights bob about on his head.

LINDA: (*noticing*) Are those my tights?

PHIL: (*lying*) No.

Linda snatches the tights off Phil's head.

PHIL: Ow! (*Rubs his head in pain*)

LINDA: They are. (*Examining the tights*) They're my Marks and Spencer's Ultimate Magic Secret Supports. They're six quid a pair. I'll kill you if you've laddered them.

PHIL: I thought you were watching 'Ocean's Eleven'.

LINDA: (*finding an eye hole*) Oh, you have - look! (*Finding a second hole, she pushes her fingers through and wiggles them at him*)

Beat. **Linda** *looks up from the tights and notices Phil's battered face. She gasps, and reaches towards his face to take a closer look.*

PHIL: (*turning away*) I'm OK.

LINDA: (*trying to see his face*) Have you been beaten up?

PHIL: No.

LINDA: (*rubbing his bruised face affectionately*) Who did this?

PHIL: Ow!

LINDA: Look at the state of you.

PHIL: (*bursts into tears*) I bloody love you... (*Sobs*)

LINDA: Are you in trouble?

Phil sobs.

LINDA: (*holds him*) Oh, Phil... (*Comforting him*) It's all right - me and Morris'll sort them out. (*She brandishes the pot, like a warrior*)

PHIL: I've made such a mess of everything. (*Sobs*)

LINDA: It doesn't matter.

PHIL: I'm so sorry... (*Sobs*)

LINDA: (*gently helping him*) Come on, you silly sod, it's freezing out here...

PHIL: (*sobbing*) I don't deserve you.

LINDA: No, you don't. Now, come on... (*Leads him towards the edge of the roof*)

PHIL: (*crying*) I didn't mean to do it.

LINDA: I know, love...

PHIL: She made me.

LINDA: Who did?

PHIL: Julie.

LINDA: (*stops*) The girl who found my necklace?

Phil nods, crying.

LINDA: I don't... (*Realising*) Christ, Philip! Are you having an affair?

Beat.

PHIL: It's over, honestly. I haven't seen her for months – apart from today - but that wasn't... I mean, I didn't ask her/to...

LINDA: (*exploding*) You bastard! (*Throws the tights at him*)

*The tights hit **Phil** in the face. **Linda** runs at him. **Phil** tries to fend off her blows and almost loses his footing, grabbing hold of her and narrowly avoiding a fall. Search lights suddenly swirl around the roof, then focus on them. **Phil** and **Linda** continue to fight, illuminated by the searchlight.*

VOICE: (*over loudhailer*) Come down from the roof. Come down from the roof.

***Phil** and **Linda** continue to fight.*

VOICE: (*over loudhailer, more insistently*) Come down from the roof.

***Phil** and **Linda** freeze, blinking into the light. They cling to each other, trying to see below them through the blinding light.*

LINDA: Oh, God! I rang the police!

PHIL: What did you do that for?

LINDA: You're hardly in a position to start blaming me. (*In her anger, almost losing her footing*)

PHIL: I know, I... (*Grabbing her*) Careful, love...

LINDA: (*trying to push him off*) Don't you 'love' me.

There is a tussle between **Linda** *and* **Phil**, *during which Phil seems to fare worse. The voice over the loudhailer speaks over the tussle.*

PHIL: Ow!

VOICE: (*over loudhailer*) Let the hostage go. Let the hostage go or we will be forced to call for armed back up.

LINDA: (*puts her hand up to shield her eyes and calls down*) No, I'm not/a...

VOICE: (*over loudhailer*) Let the hostage go.

LINDA: (*calling down, waving*) I'm not a hostage. (*To Phil*) They can't hear me. (*Shouting louder and waving*) Hello! Hello! (*Louder*) I'm not a hostage.

PHIL: I don't want you to die, Linda.

LINDA: Will you shut up.

PHIL: (*fervently*) I don't want you to die.

LINDA: You're really not helping.

PHIL: (*sobbing*) But...

LINDA: No one's going to die, Philip. We're on top of our shed, not up the Eiffel Tower.

PHIL: (*stepping forward, in despair*) I was only going to burgle the house. I wasn't/going to...

LINDA: Burgle the house?

PHIL: (*looking down over the edge of the roof*) Mmm...

LINDA: But you live here. You've got a key.

Phil leans forward, still peering over the edge. He is in his own world.

LINDA: What are you doing?

VOICE: (*over loudhailer*) Come down from the roof. Come down from the roof.

LINDA: Phil – look at me. (*Beat*) Look at me, Philip.

PHIL: When I was a kid I used to stand next to this picture in assembly. 'Icarus' it was called.

LINDA: Look at me, Phil.

PHIL: That fella with the wings.

LINDA: I know who Icarus was.

PHIL: It was like another world. Perfect green sea... A boat with big billowing sails. And the sky filled with all this... sunshine...

LINDA: (*peering nervously below her*) Phil, this is hardly the time...

PHIL: And there were sheep. And some fella ploughing a field. (*Laughing to himself*) He was quite funny actually... (*Laughs to himself, in his own world*)

LINDA: Phil/...?

PHIL: And in the middle of all this... scenery... were these little white legs disappearing into the green water. (*Makes a 'flailing' gesture with his fingers, then smiles at her sadly*) There's no money left.

LINDA: I don't...

PHIL: It's all gone.

LINDA: But your promotion..?

PHIL: I lied, Linda. I lied - I'm in loads of debt. (*Pause*) I've let you down.

LINDA: Yes, you have.

PHIL: (*in his own world*) And it's so much money... But I wanted.../I wanted to...

LINDA: I don't give a shit about the money.

PHIL: (*leans closer to the edge, peering down*) Just say I fell.

LINDA: What are you doing?

PHIL: They'll only pay out if they think it's an accident.

LINDA: Oh, now you're just being silly.

Phil stretches out his arms, as if to fly.

LINDA: Phil!

VOICE: (*over loudhailer*) Come down from the roof. (*Beat*) Come down from the roof.

PHIL: Don't worry, Lind. Everything's going to be all right. (*He leans forward to throw himself off the shed roof*)

LINDA: (*shouts*) Phil!

Blackout.

LINDA: (*screams*) Phil!

The sound of sirens swells in the darkness.

EPILOGUE

Nan sits rocking in the rocking chair. The table beside her contains her usual paraphernalia – skulls, paper and flashing devils. She talks directly to the audience.

NAN: (*laughs*) I can see the headline now - 'Big-eared bugger bounces.' (*Laughs to herself*) Well, he only threw himself off the shed roof, so the silly sod didn't die. He'd two fractured ribs, a broken tibia - and a crown. And fuck knows where he got the money for that 'cos good dental work don't come cheap these days. (*Laughs*) Bet he ain't feeling so easy now, clutching his crutches and waiting for my knock on the door. But it's like that computer game - Final Fantasy - when your time's up it's up. (*Laughs*)

Phil is stretchered off, groaning. Linda walks with the stretcher, holding his hand. She is wrapped in a foil blanket. Nan watches them go.

NAN: She's up the duff by the way - 'Linda' - in case you hadn't guessed. She don't know it yet, but her fondest dreams have come true at last. (*Dramatically*) 'What a miracle! However did that happen?' Well, it weren't magic, if that's what you're thinking. (*Laughs dirtily*) Probably all them strawberries they've been shovelling into their greedy gobs. No,

I'm pleased for 'em, I really am. Couldn't happen to a nicer pair. (*Beat*) They'll need to borrow more money now of course. But I've always fancied a young boy on my team, so I'm sure we can come to some sort of arrangement. And then we'll live happily ever after. (*Laughs to herself*)

You little people with your little lives and your debt and your need and your pain. Can't stop yourselves, can you, when you're heading for a fall. (*Shakes her head, laughing to herself*) You feel it deep inside, like a knife in your gut 'cos you know you deserve more than this. And you 'covet'. Isn't that the phrase they use when they're trying to warn you off? 'Thou shalt not covet lest you let the devil in' – or some old bollocks. (*laughs*) Only it ain't bollocks, is it – you know that now. 'Cos one day you will covet something way beyond your grasp. Covet it so bad you'd sell your soul. And on that day, sure as Euros is Euros, and pounds is pounds - on that day, I'll be there.

Nan grins as the lights fade, leaving only the little devils and skulls lit on the stage, flashing merrily in their various and changing colours.

Into: The Smiths – 'Heaven Knows I'm Miserable Now'.

APPENDIX – LATIN, ACT 1 SCENE 4

inter alia – among other things
de facto – in fact, in reality
ergo - therefore
pro rata - proportionally
pacta sunt servandi – promises must be kept
bona fide – genuine, real
ad quod damnum – according to the harm
condicio sine qua non - [a condition] without which it could not be or without which [there is] nothing.
ad vitare dubium – for the avoidance of doubt
peine forte et dure - for hard and forceful punishment
ignorantia juris non excusat - ignorance of the law does not excuse
in terrorem – to frighten
cuius est solum eius est usque ad coelum et ad inferos – to whom is the soil, it is theirs up to Heaven and down to Hell
consummatum est – it is completed

Libera Me – from the Requiem Mass:

Deliver me from eternal death on that terrible day,
When the heavens and the earth shall be moved,
When you shall come to judge the world by fire.
I am made to tremble, and I fear, the judgement that

will come, and the coming wrath,
When the heavens and the earth shall be moved.
That day, the day of wrath, calamity, and misery, the day of great and exceeding bitterness,
When you shall come to judge the world by fire.
Eternal rest grant unto them: and let light perpetual shine upon them.